90 Lessons

for

Living Large

in

90 Square Feet

(...or more)

Here are a few of the many emails written to Felice from strangers in response to the YouTube video of her 90-square-foot studio

"I really enjoyed the exhaustive YouTube apartment tour, but what I love even more is your amazing adventure and your positive outlook."

— California

"I watched a video clip about your 90 sq. ft. I always try to declutter but now I see my place getting stuffed with unnecessary things… moving stuff up sounds like a good idea. How do you do it? Its great! So cozy and everything is organized. Would appreciate any advice on how to organize my living space. Thank you for your video."

— Croatia

"Being frustrated because of my unorganized studio apartment in Portland, Maine, I typed into Google: 'beautiful organized interiors.' Thus finding your YouTube. Thanks for the inspiration. Now to get to work eliminating clutter, etc."

— Maine

"I saw your story on a Greek site here. Believe me you are lucky because you have the chance to live in this beautiful place. You organized really good your small space… and if you will write a book I really want it. Smile every day and take care."

— Greece

"I saw your video on how you organized your apt. You're a true inspiration to me. I wish I could have the gene that you do that makes you organized. I hope one day you'll have a DVD/meditation/life improvement instructional video on how to organize your life."

— Spain

"I'm working towards separating myself from possessions and towards people, experiences, and my writing. Thank you for the inspiration!"

— Tennessee

"I saw your video, very impressive. You're real. Bold and smart. You did inspire me. Not because of your place but, mostly because of your optimism for life and self-confidence. Good luck."

— India

"When I saw your video I thought, I can do this. I love your energy and creativity."

— Australia

Also by Felice Cohen

What Papa Told Me (memoir)

The Fancy Tales Series
She'safella
Peter Pan Zee
Jack and the Bad Stock

Anthologies
In the Shadows of Memories
The Truth About the Fact
To Daddy, With Love

90 Lessons
for
Living Large
in
90 Square Feet
(...or more)

Felice Cohen
Dividends Press

90 Lessons for Living Large in 90 Square Feet (…or more)

First Edition

ISBN 10: 1500657859
ISBN 13: 978-1500657857

Dividends Press

Cover design by: www.maggiecousins.com

Printed in the United States of America

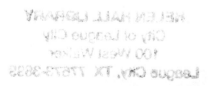

www.felicecohen.com

To Uncle Mark

For welcoming me into your home
when I needed it.
And for also kicking me out of your home
when I needed it.

"Our life is frittered away by detail. Simplify, simplify."

— **Henry David Thoreau**

"The secret of happiness, you see, is not found in seeking more, but in developing the capacity to enjoy less."

— **Socrates**

90 Lessons

for

Living Large

in

90 Square Feet

(...or more)

Introduction

I begin each morning reading my horoscope. I know a newspaper horoscope carries about as much weight as a politician's promise, but it still gives me a positive outlook on the day. Especially the day it said:

'Famous Cancers include Henry David Thoreau. Who else but a Cancer would go out into the woods, live by themselves in a small space and write a book about their feelings?"

Uh... me?

Okay, so I wasn't "in the woods," but I was deep in the center of a concrete jungle, living alone in a 90-square-foot studio in the middle of New York City and writing about it. Like Thoreau, I came to appreciate living with less.

A lot less.

From the years (1845-1847) Thoreau spent living alone in the woods in a small cabin on Walden Pond in Concord, Massachusetts, he learned that the more "stuff" we accumulate, the more we are forced to be custodians of these things and this excess is not only bad for us, but also inflames the appetite for more. After five years of living in a tiny space on the fifth floor of a former tenement building on the Upper West Side, I had arrived at the same conclusion: I had grown accustomed to an independence from stuff. Along the way, my fantasies of "one day" living in a large home with a voluminous foyer illuminated by skylights, had changed too. Instead, they were now of living with just the space I actually needed, preferably near a bike path.

When I eventually showcased that independence–and my lean, mean, 12' x 7.5' Manhattan studio–on YouTube, the video went viral. It landed on Yahoo's home page and in one day got over one million hits. Friends I hadn't talked to in years messaged me on Facebook. Strangers from China, Croatia, India, Israel, Italy, London, Pakistan, Poland, Texas, Wisconsin and other places sent me a flood of emails (including a few dating proposals) to say how much they admired the steps I took to transform this small space and my philosophy about "living large" in that space.

Along with emails came phone calls from *Good Morning America*, *The Ellen DeGeneres Show*, *The Nate Berkus Show*, and TV and radio stations in Australia, Brazil, Canada, Germany, Ireland and South Korea. I was interviewed for dozens of Internet and newspaper articles, and hundreds of other sites reposted the original video–all totally unexpected. Meanwhile, I tried to answer hundreds of emails, started a Facebook fan page, opened a Twitter account, and created the blog *Living Large in Any Space.*

It was only after hearing repeated requests for details on "how you did it" that the idea arose for this book. But bookstore shelves are already filled with such books, and the last thing I wanted was to add another "how-to" guide to the serious book clutter out there. My solution: share the techniques I've developed over the years (as a born neat freak and, later, as a professional organizer) and the lessons I learned from overcoming the limits of a small space–the arranging, consolidating and simplifying–that made my tiny apartment feel many times bigger.

Therefore, this book is less a "how to" guide and more a "want to" guide to help motivate and inspire you to arrange the life you want. Whether that's a smaller space to care for, fewer distractions, finding a "home" for all your stuff or spending more time enjoying life is up to you. Whatever your goal, this book can help get you there.

How I Came to Live in 90 Square Feet

I grew up on Cape Cod, the skinny peninsula off the state of Massachusetts shaped like an arm flexing its bicep. My childhood bedroom was 17' x 17' with two large walk-in closets that I reorganized for fun. It never dawned on me that I could (or would) eventually make a living organizing other people's closets.

In high school, for extra credit, I organized my French teacher's storage closet ("magnifique!") and my friends' closets during sleepovers ("wicked cool!"). While an undergraduate at the University of Massachusetts Amherst, I occasionally organized dorm rooms in exchange for slices of pizza. But it was during my senior year, in a sports marketing course, that I realized how valuable my organizing abilities could be. My professor, aware of my proclivity for order, asked if

I would be interested in organizing the office at the Volleyball Hall of Fame in Holyoke, Massachusetts for extra credit. Having been recruited to play Division I volleyball and softball my freshman year, I looked forward to seeing the museum–that is until I saw its messy miniscule back office. Boxes spilling over with deflated volleyballs, Olympics memorabilia, documents, books and office supplies filled virtually every inch of space. Where to begin? It looked like an impossible task. But I knew, from all the organizing I had done in my life, that in every pile of stuff there's a pattern waiting to be discovered. Spot it and you're on your way to the finish line.

Within moments I saw a paper clip on the floor. Then another. And another. I grabbed a chipped coffee mug and began filling it with paper clips. I had found the pattern and was on my way.

Hours later, trash eliminated, files created and items grouped, boxed and labeled, the space appeared to double in size. After that, my professor hired me to organize his garage.

Following graduation, with dreams of becoming a writer, I began interviewing my maternal grandfather, a Holocaust survivor, to write a book about his experiences in the war. (He had been in eight different labor and concentration camps.) To pay the bills, I had a day job working in Admissions at my alma mater, recruiting, planning events and helping to create and run orientation sessions for 4,500 new students every summer. I was also organizing closets on the side for extra cash.

During that time I caught a segment on the *Today* show about a woman in New York City who made her living as a professional organizer. That was my "Aha!" moment. *I could do that*, I thought. Plus, Manhattan is where writers live. So thanks to an offer from my uncle Mark to live with him in his Bronx apartment, I gave away my furniture, stuffed my clothes, computer and bicycle into my Honda Accord, and headed south.

Once settled in New York, I found a professional organizing company in the phone book (no Google at the time) and showed up unannounced at a tiny bright studio office whose shelves were neatly stacked with identically labeled white storage boxes. The owner, a bit surprised I had appeared without an appointment, arranged for a "hands on" interview to test my organizing skills.

We met the next morning at a one-bedroom apartment in a high-rise building near Wall Street. Dirty laundry, piles of mail and magazines, books, old take-out containers, sweatshirts, towels and random shoes covered every surface, including the floor. Just like at the Volleyball Hall of Fame, I found my starting point (the shoes) and began. When my potential boss found me sitting on the floor of the bedroom closet arranging pairs of men's shoes so that every other shoe faced the opposite direction (to maximize space) she said, "That's exactly what I do! You're hired." Then, before leaving me to finish the job, she added, "The client has some sensitive items. If you find them, just leave them where they are."

A few hours later, when I was about to leave, I noticed the hall closet door wouldn't close. There was a dresser inside sticking out, blocking the track. I leaned over the dresser and found a black leather duffle bag wedged behind it. I removed the bag, pushed the dresser back and slid the door shut. Then I opened the bag to see the contents so I'd know where to put them. Inside were handcuffs and a whip. Ah yes, the "sensitive" items. I reversed my steps and left, leaving the hall closet door ajar.

Over the next several years I organized apartments and offices in all five boroughs, even New Jersey and Connecticut, though mostly in Manhattan. Some jobs lasted an afternoon; others weeks. Clients included a billionaire, a supermodel, a television personality, a rock star, a fashion designer, even a Broadway lyricist, plus plenty of regular folks, all needing order in their busy lives. There was the older woman in the small, dingy studio in the West Village overlooking Washington Square Park with an addiction to catalogs and Smarties; the family with two sons who lived in a brownstone on the Upper West Side with an indoor basketball court on the top floor; and the hoarder on the East Side who was against experimentation on lab rats and had over 100 of them crammed in stacked glass fish tanks in the middle of her equally as scary messy living room.

Of course the tasks were just as varied–everything from cleaning out basement storage units to unpacking entire families into duplex apartments to categorizing the home library of the son of a famous catalog magnate. I once spent an afternoon in a gigantic loft overlooking Union Square, refolding a client's underwear and towels into perfect squares.

A few years later, I began to re-focus on the reason I moved to New York City in the first place: to write. I got a job as the assistant to the Editorial Page Editor at the New York *Daily News*. Aside from organizing the office, creating a working filing system and overseeing all administrative details, I had three Op/Eds published. A year later, I left the *Daily News* to help launch *Next Zone*, a women's sports magazine that was the official magazine of the New York Liberty and other teams in the WNBA. Unfortunately, issues with our venture capitalist forced us to shutter our hip office in SoHo and soon I was back to organizing closets.

But not for long.

I had received a phone call from the newly appointed president of the City of New York's Hunter College (and wife of my ex-boss from the *Daily News.)*

"After hearing how you organized everything at the paper," she said. "I'd love you to come run my office."

So at 32, I became Chief of Staff to a college president. I often worked 12-hour days, overseeing a staff of eight, organizing events and acting as the liaison between the president and every dean, professor, staff member, alumnus and student who wanted the president's ear. It was a demanding job, but there were perks. I met Bill Clinton, Al Sharpton, Christine Todd Whitman, Michael Bloomberg, Rhea Perlman, Ellen Barkin, Cynthia Nixon, Ruby Dee, Alan Alda and others when they visited campus. Some even talked with me about their closets.

As the fourth anniversary of my position as Chief of Staff grew near, my dream of becoming a full-time writer was once again petitioning for my full attention. (In my spare time, I had been filing weekly Op-Ed pieces for the New York City newspaper, *amNew York*, and working with my maternal grandfather on finishing the book we had started years before.) I found myself staring out the window of my sunny 17th floor office, daydreaming about quitting my job. But then I'd think about my rent and other expenses that kept me (as it does millions of others) tethered to a steady paycheck with health benefits.

At the same time, another itch flared up. After living in the Bronx for years, I yearned to be a part of that Living in Manhattan Club and would stare longingly at the walkers, runners and cyclists enjoying Central Park from my seat on the Express bus. Even though I made a decent salary and had been diligently saving, the thought of pouring my money into paying a high rent seemed wrong. I couldn't take the plunge. At least not on my own.

On the evening of December 31, 2006, my uncle muted the TV's New Year's Eve celebration. "I'm glad we had the chance to live together," Mark said. "But it's time for us to live on our own. How's April first?" Three months away. In New York City apartment-speak, that's like three seconds.

I looked first at studios on the Upper East Side, because the realtor said it was more affordable. But most faced the backs of other sunless studios.

One day a friend I hadn't spoken to in years, called out of the blue. "Still living in the Bronx?" she asked.

"Yes," I told her. "But I have to move."

"Where are you looking?"

"I'd love the Upper West Side, but it is way out of my price range," I said.

"I know someone looking to sublet her studio on the Upper West Side, but it's small," she warned. "If Michael Jordan were to reach both arms out, he could touch opposite walls." Surely she was exaggerating. But so what? I was a huge Michael Jordan fan.

Two days later, I was climbing 70 creaky steps to a fifth-floor apartment just off Columbus Avenue. When Lara, the woman subletting the studio, opened the door, the first thing I saw was a two-burner electric stovetop covered in equal amounts of rust and cat hair. Cautiously, I stepped inside. Or tried to. There wasn't much room inside the 12' x 7.5' studio, which was jam-packed with stuff. Next to the unsightly burner was a mini fridge, smaller than the one I had in college.

Adjacent to that was a table obscured by a mound of paper, magazines and newspapers.

Across from this mess was the closet. Situated behind two hollow sliding doors (which fell off their tracks when I opened them), was the classic shelf-perched-over-a-clothing-rod, the most impractical design for closets.

Next to the closet was the bathroom, which was incredibly narrow. There wasn't much room between the tub, the miniature sink and the toilet, which (as I would later joke on the YouTube video), if you had long legs required sideways sitting, otherwise your knees would bang against the tub.

On the other side of the room, bulky bookcases stood on either side of the room's only window. In front of them a futon was folded up into its couch position, blocking the one redeeming quality of the apartment: a brick wall. It also blocked the bottom rungs of a steep ladder that led up to a narrow loft bed. (The loft bed was the most commented-on part of my YouTube video; many wondered if it was possible to be intimate with someone up there. For the record, it was.)

Standing midway up the ladder I noticed the limited headspace between the mattress and the ceiling. I pulled out a tape measure. Twenty-three inches. I measured it again. Same result–a distance so small that unless you were under the age of four you could not sit up in the bed. I moved to get on the bed to try lying down when I caught sight of Lara's cat (the source of the hair coating almost everything) curled up in a far corner looking displeased I was encroaching on its space.

"Looks okay," I said, backing down the ladder.

"Aren't you going to try lying down?" Lara said. "To make sure you're okay with it."

Eyeing the cat eyeing me, I said, "I slept on top bunks at camp. How bad can it be?"

Famous last words.

"So," said Lara, when I'd stepped off the ladder onto the futon and then onto the floor. "Interested?"

I looked around the cramped quarters. As an organizer, I'd transformed dozens of messy apartments (albeit all larger than this one) and had made them livable. Certainly I could do that here. But that bed. I looked back up at it, then over at Lara. She was almost six feet tall and said her boyfriend was taller. I was five feet three inches. If they had no problem sleeping up there... Plus, at $700 a month, the rent wouldn't be a drain on my savings, which meant I could quit my job and finish my grandfather's book.

"I'll take it," I said.

I spent the next month preparing for the move. Since I could only bring in about an eighth of my belongings, I gave some stuff away and put the rest into storage, figuring I'd get it after my year in Manhattan. I quit my job. It was April 2007. Change was in the air.

As I followed the movers up the stairs and into my new home, the studio looked even smaller than I'd remembered. I quickly chalked it up to the presence of the tall, muscular moving guys and the stacks of boxes occupying the 90 square feet.

(What is 90 square feet? Imagine the perimeter of a 2001 Honda Accord. That was the size of my new home. I know this because I had drawn the apartment layout in chalk on the driveway of my parents' Cape Cod home the week before the move. Then, for fun, I pulled my car into the outline. It fit perfectly.)

When the movers were done, Lara handed me the keys, wished me luck and left. Alone with my stuff, I sat on the window ledge and looked around. After a moment of quiet contemplation that I was, for the first time in years, in a room all my own, I got to work.

But my usual professional-unpacking routine–first empty every box–wasn't going to work. There wasn't enough room. I needed a new plan. My ultimate goal was to keep the one brick wall clutter free, and to do that I bought three sets of adjustable steel shelving units from the Container Store and Ikea to hold most of my stuff. Everything would be going up, up, up.

The bottom shelf of the largest unit would be my desk and the others would house stuff-filled totes, which I labeled: Toiletries, Electronics, Hats and Gloves, and so on. Only then did I empty my moving boxes, sorting the contents directly into the totes. When all the packing boxes were emptied, I hoisted the totes onto the shelves, and suddenly the room was larger.

Then I tackled the closet. Closets have always been my favorite organizing challenge. I removed the two hollow wooden doors from the track, wrapped them in an old white bed sheet and stuck them in the narrow unused space between the tub and the bathroom wall. (In all the years I lived in the apartment, I barely noticed them.) In their place I hung a tension rod with a curtain I could pull back for a view of everything inside.

On the top shelf I placed folded piles of pajamas, T-shirts and sweaters. I attached a drop-down adjustable closet rod on the left side of the existing closet rod, increasing my hanging space by almost 50 percent. I hung all pants and skirts on this bottom bar, leaving the top rod for shirts–arranged in short-sleeved, long-sleeved and blazer groups, a helpful way to put together outfits.

Next I assembled a 25-slot shoe cubby for the bottom right side of the closet. Cubbies are a great way to store shoes. The slots are also perfect for umbrellas and yoga mat storage.

Once finished with the closet, I went for a walk in my new neighborhood, taking in the restaurants, markets, boutiques, yoga studios, movie theaters and museums. I felt as though I'd moved into a better residential area on an urban campus. Then, with sushi and a gallon of water in hand, I headed home for my first night in the loft bed.

After vacuuming out the cat hair and scrubbing down the area with bleach, I set up the "bedroom" inside the narrow enclave. I laid down a new mattress and a headboard shelf to house my writing journals, radio alarm clock and copy of Henry David Thoreau's *Walden*. Then I made the bed. Ever make a bed while on top of it on your hands and knees? It would make Houdini proud.

I had asked my friend Ann to sleep over, as I was scared I might slip off the ladder or tumble out of the loft. (She slept on the open side near the railing.) I fell asleep quickly, exhausted from the day, but woke in the middle of the night drenched in sweat.

"I have to get out!" I yelled, disoriented and feeling trapped by the walls, ceiling and even by Ann's proximity. I flew down the wooden ladder, missing half the rungs and banging my shins on the others. "What was I thinking?" I paced every available inch of the small apartment. My leg muscles were on fire from climbing the stairs so many times the day before. "Did I make a huge mistake? That bed is ridiculous! What if I need to get out in an emergency? Not to mention all those stairs!"

"Breathe," Ann coaxed. "Use your yoga breaths."

"Screw my yoga breaths! I've moved into a place with a coffin for a bed!"

I eventually calmed down, unrolled a yoga mat onto the floor and lay on my back with my arms and legs spread out, careful not to bang them on the desk chair, shelves or the wall, while also trying to ignore the lingering smell of cat pee emanating from behind the base of the ladder. (The next place to scrub, I thought sleepily).

"You made the right decision," Ann said, dropping down a pillow for me. "You can add a handle to the side of the ladder to make it easier to get out. And don't forget, you're living your dream. You're a writer in Manhattan."

In all my unpacking I had forgotten about my reason for moving in the first place. That was when I had another "Aha!" moment. For the next 12 months I would have to live in 90 square feet as well as walk up five flights. All this would require some major adjustments. Well, really, just one.

My attitude.

Everything I needed to live in New York City was within reach (literally). If I had a positive outlook I would be fine. From that moment on I considered the stairs an exercise bonus rather than a burden. Extra calories burned daily. As for those 90 square feet? A professional opportunity. What better way to improve upon my organizing chops? Plus, with fewer expenses, I could work less and have more time to write. It was only for a year, I reminded myself. It would be worth it.

And it was.

During that first year I grew accustomed–physically and mentally–to the small space. And with my low rent, I had enough money to join Paragraph, a writer's studio in Chelsea, where I finished writing my grandfather's book. I was able to afford travel and, without a demanding job, attend Broadway matinees and ride my bicycle on a whim.

Moving into that space–in spitting distance of Lincoln Center and Central Park–had been the ultimate challenge. And when that first year came to an end, I wasn't ready to leave. So I told Lara, who was living in another part of the state, that I wanted to stay for another year. That year turned into another. And another. And another. I may have been living in a small space, but I was, without a doubt, living large.

90 Lessons
for
Living Large
in
90 Square Feet
(...or more)

1

Getting organized is as **easy** as:

- One (toss)
- Two (categorize)
- Three (put away)

2

The Only Way to Begin Is to Begin

Pick a starting point, like your sock drawer or belts or kitchen spice rack, and just work on that. Even a little dent makes a difference. Like Newton's Law of Inertia, an object in motion (in this case: you) will stay in motion once you simply begin.

3

First thing every morning, **make your bed**. It sets a productive intention to your day.

4

Lather. Rinse. Repeat.

We all know that when you make pancakes, the first one usually comes out lumpy, burnt or falls apart. That's because you're trying to get the batter consistency and temperature just right. After that first pancake, you usually get in the groove and thereafter each pancake comes out better. The same is true when you organize. You may unpack your kitchen and put the coffee mugs near the coffee maker. But after a week you realize it would be better to have them near the dishwasher, so you move the mugs. Organizing is not always a "one and done" process, sometimes you need to tweak it to get it just right.

5

Store a complete set of bed sheets inside one of its own pillowcases. Then you'll never search for a matching set again.

6

To-Do or Not To-Do Lists

A To-Do list–written on a notepad or tapped into your smart phone–gives you structure and direction. Whether you're preparing for a kitchen renovation, a wedding or just trying to get stuff done, a list is not only essential, it adds a certain dignity and value to these tasks. Lists also free up mental space otherwise used to remember everything you need to do. And crossing items off as they're completed will provide you with a sense of achievement. Best of all, lists capture life's moments, and just looking at those crossed-off tasks may help you appreciate how accomplished you really are.

7

Preparation prevents aggravation.

8

Better 10 Minutes Early than One Minute Late

Being a professional organizer in New York City, I travel everywhere by foot, subway or bus. Clients are downtown and uptown, on the east side and the west. Wherever I'm going, I make it a point to be 10 minutes early, which avoids unnecessary stress and ensures that I'm always on time. When you're late, you're implying that your time is more important than anyone else's, something that I know my clients (or friends) would not appreciate. The key to not being late is, of course, to be prepared: your outfit laid out the night before, keys by the door, weather forecast checked, directions ready. And the key to being prepared? Being organized.

9

If you fail, don't beat yourself up, **pick yourself up**. Try again.

10

Don't Ever Put Your Clothes Away*

*If you're not going to do it right.

While I'm a firm believer in "put it back where it belongs," there are some exceptions. Like if you're too tired or too busy to do it correctly. To keep your closet and dresser neat, hold off from putting anything away–whether it's something you wore that day or a basket of clean laundry–until you've got the time and energy to put the clothes away neatly and in the right spot. Putting them away haphazardly sabotages your hard work. Remember, how your clothes look in the closet is an indication of how they are going to look on you. Messy closet? Messy you. Neat closet? Neat you.

11

Whatever it is, **get over it.**

12

(Re)Solutions

Millions of us make New Year's resolutions and promptly ignore them. Why? A date on the calendar is not going to motivate you to do what you haven't done during the previous 365 days. A resolution is not a wish, but a promise to begin and complete something. To keep that resolution, you need a solution. Creating a time line of manageable steps can make a daunting goal less intimidating. Maybe try month by month, or use holidays as benchmarks–Valentine's Day, Fourth of July, Thanksgiving. If you want to organize your home, you may not have 12 rooms, but 12 areas that need work–kitchen, linen closet, garage–so plan to tackle one area each month. It's like purchasing a bookcase from Ikea: You don't open the box and find the item assembled. You find a list of steps. The same with a resolution. To get the best results, take it step-by-step.

Happy New You!

13

"Aha!" moments are rare gifts of insight. Follow up on those intuitions. **Trust** your gut.

14

Pro...Cras...Ti...Na...Tion

The problem with putting things off to the last minute is that the last minute arrives more quickly than we expect. Deadline, as the word implies, can feel like a life or death moment, but it doesn't have to. In fact, it can help motivate you. Since the hardest part of most assignments often is starting them, use the deadline to kindle a fire under yourself. If that doesn't work, here are three techniques I use. First, I do a yoga "breathe in, breathe out" exercise for 30 seconds to clear my chest and brain from the "deadline" pressure. Then I choose something from my To-Do list that I know I can accomplish in a short time–returning one phone call, say, or paying a bill. The simple act of crossing off a single task from my list restores confidence and energy to resume progress towards that bigger task. And if I really need a push, I promise myself a reward when the arduous task is done–a bike ride, a chai latte or a favorite TV episode. It's surprising how little sparklers can ignite great sparks.

15

Just as you schedule time for meetings, schedule time to organize. Even **five minutes makes a difference**.

16

Organize for Your Health

An important factor in our well-being is reducing stress. Time (or lack of it) is often a major source of stress. So how do we get more time? Simple. By finding what you need when you need it. This can add minutes and even hours to your day. And how do you find stuff faster? By not having so much of it. Having less stuff to sort through also means you'll spend less time cleaning stuff, putting stuff away, picking stuff up and working to pay for all that stuff. Then with all that extra time, who knows what fun things you'll get to do, like, say, relax, which can, like, you know, ease your stress.

17

Make the **most use** of
[ ] space.
Store off-season
clothing under the bed
or shelve out an entire
wall.

18

From Buy! Buy! To "Buh-Bye!"

The first concept I introduce to each new client is how to say, "Buh-bye" to some possessions. Sure it's easy to say, but it's *how* you say it that counts. It helps to have the following attitude, such as, "Object X, you've lost your significance and are no longer worth taking up my valuable space. *Buh-bye*!" Most clients follow me fearlessly into the battle against the clutter monster and end up joyously saying, "buh-bye!" when filling bags for donation or trash. Some clients are not quite sure whether my "buh-bye!" system is a joke or a serious strategy. The answer is: both. My aim is to add a lighter tone to what can often be an emotional challenge. More than one client has cried as they consigned worn clothing, dust-covered paperbacks or old pocketbooks onto the giveaway pile. Many have also shed tears of joy and relief after we've finished.

19

Keep an **open mind**. Shutting yourself off from something new or different may keep you from reaching your goal sooner.

20

Bought Something New? Discard Something Used.

I have an "In and Out" philosophy when it comes to your possessions that is similar to the "Take a penny, leave a penny" sign at many small-store counters. Each time you acquire something new that is similar to an item you already own–clothes, linens, lipstick, tools, shoes, pots–get rid of the older item ASAP. Applying this simple principle to your stuff keeps your home looking neat. Now, of course, if the item you are replacing is still in good condition, why are you buying another?

21

Leave a room **neater** than it was when you entered it. (Especially if it's not your room.)

22

Fall into Step

Each autumn, clear blue skies and crisp cool breezes bring me back to the feel of a new school year–that sense of a new beginning. I especially loved getting blank notebooks, knowing that by the end of the semester they would be filled with the knowledge that had led me to my goal: passing the course. However, the fall after my college graduation, I felt lost. So my dad bought me a new notebook.

"What's this for?" I asked.

"For your next course," he said. "Beginning a life: 101."

"But I have no syllabus to follow," I said.

"Create your own," he advised. "Write down your goals and the outline to get you there."

I've been following that advice ever since. Whether you want to organize your garage or create an app, something as simple as a notebook can help you stay focused until you reach your goal.

23

Even **baby steps**
are steps forward.

24

Way to Go!

In major league baseball, most every play, whether successful or not, results in a high five. This simple gesture of acknowledgment says, "Good job!" and instills confidence and motivation. How many of us receive that feedback at work?

"Hey Lenny, great job on the mailing! High five!"

Not many.

As we get older, where does the motivation to show up at work, cook dinner, and floss regularly come from? Maybe our current addiction to Facebook reflects less about "sharing" and more about getting feedback to acknowledge the value of our mundane work. When I write, I keep a picture of an open palm nearby. Then every time I need a little encouragement, there's a high five waiting.

25

Don't sit up **too quickly** in bed.

26

Maybe Peter Pan Was on to Something

Ever watch little kids approach a playground? They race to get there, usually hollering with delight. What was the last thing you sprinted toward? The midnight sale at Target after Thanksgiving? Children may not understand the value of play, but they certainly benefit from it. Schools have recess because it's an opportunity for a necessary release. As adults we no longer have "recess," but we do have lunch breaks and vacation days, though many of us do not even take them. As we get older, that need for "play" is still critical, and not taking a break from work will leave us tired and stressed. How fun is that?

27

Holding on to stuff can hold you back. **Let it go**.

28

All Kidding Aside

Involving kids in organizing their play area makes them more likely to keep it neat. Here are some tips that help:

- Avoid grumpy hour.
- Explain to kids their donations will help another child. Kids may be small, but they have big hearts.
- Choose one concentration at a time–books, games, puzzles, dolls–and dump it all out on the floor. Toss anything that's missing parts, bag items no longer played with for donation, and gather small pieces into Ziplocs.
- Use containers with covers.
- Put puzzles, toys and games into their own separate container, and label with words, pictures or actual pieces. Ask the kids to make the labels.
- Have the children roll a pair of dice. The total number is how many items to discard.

29

E X P A N D

your **Comfort Zone**. Order something new from the menu or take a different route to work. When we step outside of our comfort zone, we're not really going out of it, we're just making it bigger.

30

Same Old Same Old

We are creatures of comfort, and often stick to routines because changes–big or small–disrupt that comfort. Take for instance, Saturday morning routines. There is nothing wrong with going to the dry cleaners, stopping at the bank and picking up groceries, but what if these errands are keeping you from more enjoyable and memorable experiences, such as going on a hike or visiting a farmer's market? When you do the same task over and over, it's easy to get into a rhythm, but sometimes it's nice to try something new. You might be surprised how habit forming that can be.

31

Creating art (even doodling or coloring) is a great stress reliever.

32

Beat the Clock

Love speed dating? Try speed tossing. Set your timer to 20 or 30 minutes or even an hour and focus on one problem area: T-shirts, toys, Tupperware. When the buzzer goes off, stop. Unless, of course, you want to keep going, then by all means, reset the timer and move on to another area. This technique lulls you into the "cleaning out" process. Knowing you can stop after a short time removes the thought of spending hours on a single task and the pressure of having to get it all done at once. It also keeps you from getting burnt out and giving up. Often, once you start to see results, you're motivated to keep going.

33

Get rid of "*just in case*" items. You think you will someday need it, but you **rarely** do.

34

Common Cents

Imagine every item in your home–or in one room or on one shelf–had its original price tag on it. Now add it up. Does it equal a mortgage payment? Cable bill? Keep this amount in mind the next time you're about to buy that glazed rooster figurine for your kitchen.

Growing up as the daughter of a bankruptcy attorney, I learned about bad business decisions or unforeseen instances (like a medical emergency that can shut off income and eat up savings) and the importance of saving and not spending thoughtlessly. It was one of the reasons I moved into an inexpensive, 90-square-foot studio. That experience enabled me to save enough money (I couldn't buy stuff anyway; I didn't have room for it), to put down a deposit on my first owned (and larger) apartment. Here are some tips to keep your money growing instead of disappearing:

Weed out unused credit cards

Cut them up!

A latte a day flushes your money away

Literally.

Change is good

Handing over exact change feels as if I'm saving money and cleaning out clutter at the same time. And at the end of each day, loose coins go into a jar. (I'm still always amazed how quickly it fills up.)

No loose bills in your pocket

Those extra seconds it takes to remove your wallet to get to your cash may make you second-guess that impulse purchase. Plus, loose bills have a way of falling out of your pocket accidentally.

Photocopy all credit cards

Snap pictures of the front and back of all cards in your wallet, and email them to yourself. This will help rectify the situation quickly if your wallet is lost or stolen, since you'll have all the info immediately available.

35

Have Fun

Many people live with clutter because they're overwhelmed by the "ginormity" of the task or because they cannot get motivated to begin. Finding a way to make the job pleasurable will make you less likely to put it off. Here are some ways that can help:

Put on your favorite music

Anything that puts pep in your step.

Don't forget to laugh

I joke throughout any organizing job. Many clients have said to me, while knee deep in piles of their stuff, "You make this fun." And why shouldn't it be?

Roll the dice

Just like with kids, adults love this too. Go from room to room, or closet to closet, and roll the dice. Your total number is how many items to discard.

Have a friend over

Friends speed up the job and refresh motivation. Maybe one day you work on your place, the next on theirs.

Flip a coin

Heads: Keep! Tails: Buh-bye!

Make it a game

In the time it takes to make coffee or for the washing machine to go through its cycle, can you empty the dishwasher? Return a phone call? Cut up vegetables for the week?

36

Look on the Bright Side

In response to the YouTube video about my tiny apartment, I received emails from people around the world, some asking for organizing tips and some saying they were newly motivated to downsize their own belongings. One email was from a New Jersey man in his forties who was forced to move into a studio because of finances.

"For the past year I've been feeling depressed about the whole downsizing thing," he wrote. *"However, after watching your video I've been inspired and I am learning to appreciate my simple living."*

With all the challenges we face in our lifetime, having a positive outlook won't make the bad things go away, but they'll surely help make them easier to deal with when they happen.

37

Do laundry **less** often.
Own **more** underwear.

38

One Person's Trash Is (Not Always) Another Person's Treasure

Some of my clients live in small studios, while others live in penthouses with more closets than they know what to do with. But regardless of the size, many of them need help switching their winter and summer wardrobes. Before putting their off-season clothing into storage, we go through each item together and I help them decide whether to keep (if they wore it that season) or donate (if they didn't).

One day I left a client's three-bedroom apartment on the Upper East Side carrying a bag of men's wool sweaters to drop off for donation. Walking down Fifth Avenue I saw a homeless man on a bench just outside Central Park. "Hi," I said, handing him a royal blue Ralph Lauren sweater. "Would you like this?" He fingered the material as if checking the quality and then, after almost a minute of close inspection, handed it back.

39

. . . On the Other Hand

A downtown Manhattan church has a donation room where homeless men and women "shop" once a week for up to 10 free items. The church's mission is to help get them back on their feet by giving them presentable clothes to wear on job interviews. In preparing to write an article about the church, I volunteered on a "Women's Shopping Day" and was encouraged by the manager to ask if anyone needed help.

"I would like to find pants to match this jacket," said a woman, holding a pilled yellow blazer. Like a sales associate at Macy's, I scoured the racks in that dimly lit basement. After finding a pair close enough to her size, we looked at shoes, searching for the least scuffed pair.

"No one ever helped me shop before," she said. I thought about all the times a perky sales associate offered to get me matching colors, styles and sizes in a clean brightly lit dressing room.

At home that evening I filled a bag with 10 items from my own closet and told my friends about my experience. When I returned to the church the next week carrying my 10 items plus bags of clothing from my friends, I was pleased to hand out the new inventory to appreciative eyes.

Seeing your donations making an immediate difference can be all the motivation you need to continue thinning out the excess, not to mention it doubles the satisfaction you get from just cleaning out your closet.

40

Practice yoga (or at least **reach** for your toes) every once in a while.

41

Gave at the Office

I once had a client whose desk at work looked like a tsunami had washed over it. Jumbled stacks of old newspapers, paid bills, ketchup packets, outdated holiday cards, half-full cans of soda, even a pair of high heels made a mountain of mess. Claiming she did this to keep coworkers from snooping through her things, each morning she would have to dig deep to find her keyboard. Finally, one day she realized her productivity was suffering and hired me to come to her office and organize her desk. For those with similar "problem" desks, here are a few tips to keep your desk in working condition:

Have a single Inbox

Put all work that needs to get done in one Inbox. Go through it regularly.

Make one To-Do list

Toss random Post-Its.

Keep only the essentials on your desk

No "paid" invoices, old cups of coffee, bent paper clips, bottles of nail polish. And no shoes! Even a tape dispenser and stapler are unnecessary unless you use them often.

Create separate "homes" for projects

Use files, binders or boxes, and label them. Be specific.

Keep out only what you're working on

Everything else, move. I started practicing this in high school with homework. One subject at a time on my desk lessened the burden of seeing all the work I had to do piled high.

Utilize the last 10 minutes of your day

Put things away, file papers, toss trash and write out the next day's To-Do list.

42

Change of Address

Moving is the perfect time to gauge your "extra stuff" ratio and a great motivator for getting rid of that stuff. Starting months before your scheduled move, begin eliminating stuff. Even one item a day makes a difference. The sooner you discard what you're not taking, the easier, quicker and less expensive moving will be. Remember, every item you own will have to be removed from a shelf or a closet, packed into a box, carried down or up stairs, loaded onto a truck and driven to a new location. Then all the steps repeated in reverse. Is each thing you own worth that time, labor and cost? Imagine your new space as a clutter-free zone, and hold onto that image as you prepare to move. Here are a few more tips:

Ahead of time, pack items you're not using
Like out-of-season clothing, holiday decorations or seldom-used kitchen appliances.

Gather packing supplies

Have on hand various sized boxes, tape, markers, garbage bags, bubble wrap and newspaper. Linens are good for wrapping delicates, and luggage is great for important documents.

Label it!

Label the box of the room the item is going to, not from. This minimizes confusion and ensures that heavy items are moved only once.

Keep a "Moving" notebook

Have phone numbers of movers, cable and utility companies, and so on. Double-check that everyone is on schedule for the day of the move.

Pack an overnight bag

Pack everyone's pajamas, toothbrushes, bed sheets, blankets, pillows and the next day's outfits to make the first night and next morning less stressful.

Use up anything already opened

Toiletries and food can spill, leak or attract insects. As for cleaning supplies, fill a box with the basics to clean after the old home is emptied, then you'll have it ready for the new place. Same with snacks. Eat 'em while you work!

43

Bon Voyage

The days leading up to any trip do not need to be more hectic than they already are. If you wait to pack until the night before, chances are you'll forget something as simple as underwear or as important as your passport. (Speaking of which, do you know where your passport is right now? And is it up to date?) Identifying ahead of time what you'll need to pack–by making a list and adding to it each time you think of something–minimizes the worry of forgetting anything. Then even if you do pack the night before, all you need to do is check off the items on your list, worries eliminated. For added benefit, bring the list with you to use as a checklist before returning home. (This can help keep you from leaving yet *another* phone charger in yet *another* hotel room.) One more tip: Before traveling internationally, photocopy your passport and driver's license and carry copies with you (email copies to yourself, too) in case you're robbed. (This tip is included thanks to a mugger I met in Peru.)

44

Memories take up no room, so you can never have too many. Start collecting now.

45

My Secret to Success

Victoria has her secret and Colonel Sanders has his, but I have mine too. It's that you already know everything you need to be successful. The secret is remembering to act on what you know. Here are reminders to keep you on track to success:

State a clear goal
This way you'll know when you reach it.

Set Priorities
Do you want more money or more free time?

Don't leave things for the last minute
Unplanned interruptions are inevitable. Completing tasks ahead of time allows you to solve last-minute crises. And there are always last-minute crises.

Avoid rushing

Rushing often results in mistakes, which means you'll have to redo it.

Get back to people

People are relying on your link in the chain not breaking. Plus, it's just good manners.

Show up on time

How can you expect to get things done or be taken seriously if you're late? (I know I said this earlier, but it's worth repeating.)

Go with the flow

Things are going to go wrong. It's inevitable. Don't lose your cool. Fix it and move on.

Say thank you

Even better, write it down.

Enjoy the process

If you resent it from the start your sense of achievement will be diluted. It's your goal. Go for it!

46

Keep a notebook next to your bed. **Writing down thoughts** can make issues less intimidating than when they're competing for your attention in the middle of the night.

47

“Batteries not included.” **Plan ahead**.

48

Lucky Me

The book *The Luck Factor* by Richard Wiseman states that lucky people are extroverts, have a relaxed attitude toward life and are open to new experiences. Since that sums me up, when the lottery hit a billion dollars I put my luck to the test.

"One Mega Millions ticket, please," I said to the cashier. Tucking the receipt into my wallet, I felt like Charlie in *Willie Wonka & the Chocolate Factory*. Would this be my golden ticket? People everywhere were talking about what they'd do if they won. *I'd quit my job...I'd buy a new car...* While those things sound great, we've seen that lottery winners don't always stay happy for long. Maybe it's because they are asking the wrong question. Instead of asking, "How will winning the lottery make me happy?" they could try asking, "What makes me happy?" Then the next question should be: "Does it really require winning the lottery?" When you answer that question truthfully, you might realize that you've already won.

49

Unsubscribe
from your
www.stuff.com.

50

Purge the Past.
Make Room for the Present.

After my freshman year at college, I returned home a grown-up. Or so I felt. My childhood bedroom, filled with games, trophies and books that only the year before had seemed completely appropriate, were now officially outgrown. As I replaced my childhood stuff with my college stuff, it became clear that we all probably do this throughout our lives. Different stages–moving, graduation, marriage, divorce or retirement–brings different stuff. While the process of getting rid of stuff can be scary, it can also be liberating as we create room in our lives for newer stages and newer things.

51

The **excess** of stuff you own will weigh you down.

52

Should Is a Big Word

Saying "should" can often make you feel bad. "I really should clean out the clutter in my extra bedroom." Instead, try saying, "I'm going to turn this extra bedroom into an office." Turning a "should" into a positive action and setting an intention can help you avoid entirely the "shoulda, coulda, woulda" syndrome. Then watch how quickly the burden of having to get rid of stuff becomes more about a gratifying goal.

53

Buying necessities in bulk saves time and money. **Dedicate** one cabinet as a "back up" and keep it stocked with replacements you use most often.

54

Is Stuff Ruining Your Life?

One client, a middle-aged woman living in a large, sunny one-bedroom in Harlem, hadn't had company in years because her furniture was blanketed with books and papers from law school. Her bedroom was equally a mess, every surface covered with clothing in several sizes. We started with the clothes. (They're less taxing than paper.) I asked how long she'd been a size six. When she said eight years, I said if she did regain the weight, while those larger sizes might fit, they'd most likely be out of style. That's all it took. "Buh-bye!" went the clothes. Next we tackled the paper. She was hesitant to discard anything, fearful she might need to refer back to it. When I said, "Everything you learned is in your head, and what you forgot you can Google," she had no trouble then saying, "Buh-bye!" to the paper as well.

In two days we filled 20 garbage bags for donation and trash. With her furniture now exposed to the air, my client, tears in her eyes, thanked me for giving her back her life.

55

Eliminating clutter can feel like getting out of debt.

56

Retail Therapy: Cure or Culprit

My niece, Paige, was four when I took her to FAO Schwartz in Manhattan. As soon as we entered the enormous toy store she picked up a doll.

"I just want to carry it around in the store," she said. "I don't need to take it home. I already have dolls at home."

How many of us could enter a mall and say, "I'm just going to carry around these new shoes. I don't need them. I already have 40 pairs at home."

Many folks use retail therapy to cheer themselves up, yet the "high" that comes from a new purchase usually lasts until you get home and realize you already have one (or four) of the same item or, of course, until your credit card bill arrives.

57

How many is too many? **Too many** is too many.

58

It's Good to Want

Ever really wanted something so much you lusted after it? Like a pair of diamond earrings or a fancier car? These thoughts usually take this form: "If only I had X my life would be better." But would it really? Maybe for a minute.

When I was little, my dad told my sisters and me that "it's good to want. It builds character." At the time I thought of wanting toys as if those wants were equal to real improvement in my life. It wasn't until I lived in those 90 square feet that I truly understood what he meant. During those years, people were constantly asking me, "Don't you want a bigger apartment?" Sure, a little more space would have been great, but would it have made me happier? Not really. In fact, wanting a larger place was my incentive to work harder to achieve the goals I'd set out for myself, like finishing my first book. When I think about what I want now–health, accomplishments, good relationships–I often realize I've already got it. Toys I can always get.

59

Double bar at least one closet.

60

Why Do We Have . . .

Rooms in our homes we don't enter.

Clothes in our closets we don't wear.

Food in our cupboards we don't eat.

Appliances in our sideboards we don't use.

Books on our shelves we don't read.

Games in our cabinets we don't play.

Music in our iTunes we don't listen to.

Channels on our TV we don't watch.

And boxes in storage we've forgotten about?

Good question.

61

One thing to never get rid of: your **sense of humor.**

62

(Dis)Solving "X" Is Easy If You Know Why

Before deciding to move into what has been called one of the smallest apartments in the world, I went through my list of "residence" priorities:

- Is it located in the Upper West Side?
- Is the rent reasonable enough to allow me to quit my job and finish writing a book?
- Is it near where I want and need to frequent, like food shopping, the bank, post office, etc.?

When all answers came back "Yes" the decision was simple. The hard part I thought would be choosing which items I could bring with me. Turns out, it wasn't. The moment I secured my "why" (to experience life in The Big Apple and finish writing a book), it made leaving behind "X" (those items I'd been lugging around for years) easy. Of course a miracle happened after moving into those 90 square feet. As my stuff quotient grew smaller, my life got bigger. When your priorities are not about stuff, life has a way of giving you so much more.

63

Fatigue slows productivity. Have **snacks** on hand.

64

Stowaways

Most of us lug our stuff everywhere we go, from apartment to apartment and house to house. Moving these same unopened boxes slows us down both physically (packing, lifting, unpacking) and financially (boxes, movers, storage units).

When I moved into that tiny apartment, I put 77 boxes of stuff into storage. (I know this number exactly, because I created an inventory listing of all the belongings in each numbered box). With each year I remained in the apartment, I revisited my storage and whittled down the stuff based on my own evidence that I hadn't used it. By the time I moved out five years later, I had liberated myself of all 77 boxes.

65

Put **yourself** first. Do at least one fun thing a day.

66

Being organized is not "One Size Fits All." Find the system that works for you and **stick** with it.

67

Go vertical whenever possible.

68

Add It Up!

After my YouTube video went viral, a producer on an HGTV show contacted me, wanting a full inventory of all the stuff I had in my tiny space for a possible segment on a show. So I counted: jeans (5 pairs), boots (10 pairs), books (8), Tupperware (2), underwear (36 pairs), socks (26 pairs), shirts (32), forks (2), plates (2), Band Aids (11), towels (4), sweaters (14), Shrinky Dink art (12), glass jars (6), belts (11), hotpot (1), and so on. When I was done, I realized I still had way too much stuff and did a purge.

Most of us do not realize how much we own until it is time to move, and how much we own is often still more than we actually need.

69

Life may be short, but it's also **W I D E**. Take advantage of the width.

70

Life Is a Puzzle

When beginning a new jigsaw puzzle I first separate out the "edge" pieces and assemble the frame. Next, I create separate piles of similar colors and work on each pile before connecting them inside the frame. Of course there are straggler pieces I cannot find a home for until most of the puzzle has been completed, but every piece always has a place it belongs. This is the same way I approach organizing and unpacking a home: your home is the puzzle frame and your stuff are the pieces, each with a specific place it fits. Those items for which there is no collective place–items stacked on tables, shoved into the back of closets–are most likely items you don't use or need. Finding a place or getting rid of those items will help keep your home organized and make straightening up a cinch. Puzzle solved.

71

Eliminate empty hangers. They add clutter and invite refill.

72

Bigger Doesn't Always Mean Better

A New York City realtor friend of mine says the first question she asks new clients is, "Do you want location or size?" (Obviously, living in a studio consisting of only 90 square feet, I chose location.) Many folks, after seeing my tiny apartment, emailed me to say that for the same rent I was paying I could live elsewhere in a larger home. But I didn't want to live elsewhere; I wanted to live in Manhattan. I may have been living in a very small space, but it was nestled into one of the greatest cities in the world. And that made all the difference.

73

“Miscellaneous” is a bad 13-letter word. If you don’t know what to call it, why do you own it?

74

Ask Yourself These Questions When Deciding Whether to Keep or Discard Clothing:

- Do I love it?
- Am I keeping it out of habit?
- Will I wear it?
- Is it well made?
- Is it easy to care for?
- When's the last time I wore it?
- Would someone else appreciate it more?
- Does it match anything else I own?
- Do I have room to store it?
- Do I already own something similar?
- Does it need to be shortened or taken in?
- How would I feel if I bumped into an ex while wearing it? (This one usually does the trick.)

75

Have a hard time making decisions? Spend one day **flipping a coin**.

76

Are You Lovin' It?

Do you love everything inside your closet? When culling through clothes, instead of asking, "What don't I want?" ask instead, "What do I love?" and keep only those things. (This is also a good question to ask *before* making a purchase.) If you don't love the way something looks and feels on you, chances are you're not going to wear it and its continued presence will only block the view of the good stuff. Considering most people wear 20% of their clothing 80% of the time, there are obviously a few items you don't love (or apparently even like). As for those items you're not sure about, make it a point to wear them (weather permitting). Chances are you'll either say, "Love this!" (keep) or "This rides up in the back!" ("Buh-bye!"). Getting rid of what you don't love leaves your closet with only the things you do. And who wouldn't love a closet full of that?

77

In junk drawers, junk will sink to the bottom over time. Routinely **clean out** the bottom.

78

Hot and Cold

Some clients have a hard time keeping their homes neat after I've organized them. To help them, I came up with a simple solution, teaching them to look at the spaces in their homes as Hot Zones and Cold Zones. Hot Zones are within reach where you store items you need access to most often–jeans, snacks and drinking glasses. Cold Zones are harder-to-reach places like high cabinets or the basement, where you store items you use less often–off-season clothing, extra light bulbs or a waffle maker. With only so much space available, storing rarely used items out of the way helps keep the rooms accessible for genuine day-to-day items.

79

It's not how much you make, it's how much you spend. Practice **mindful** shopping.

80

When Push Comes to Shove

Maybe you're not planning to move next month or next year (or ever!), but take a moment to look around your home. Are there items you don't use? Don't need? Don't want? Why wait until you are forced to move to get rid of stuff that's only collecting dust? Getting rid of the stuff now lets you take the time to go through items, reflect on them and either give them to someone who may want it, need it or appreciate it more, or else you can sell the item without being desperate to do so.

81

Books are meant to be read, not to collect dust. **Donate** used books.

82

Buy One, Get One More You Don't Need

One of my clients lives alone in a four-bedroom apartment with numerous closets packed with toiletries. One day we removed every toiletry item and spread them out on her dining room table. It looked as if we had robbed CVS. We tossed anything outdated and anything she had no need for. She was amazed by the assortment of obsolete items and the money wasted. After this initial paring down we categorized what remained: first aid, grooming, dental, cosmetics. We put them in separate, labeled containers (Ziplocs also work great). The items that went into the medicine cabinet (Hot Zone) were those she used regularly. Replacements and those items used less often went back into the storage closets (Cold Zones). Remember: even though stores offer "deals" on toiletries, think twice before buying too many. They're not a bargain if they go unused.

83

Always, always, always **back up** your computer.

84

The Key To: "Where Did I Leave My Keys?"

Consistency
Keep keys in the same places at home and work.

Copy
Make a duplicate of all keys. Label them and keep them where you can find them.

Clump
Keys are used in groups, so group them together on your keychain by category–home, office, car–and have the blades face the same way.

Color Code
Make the house key blue, the office key red... It may cost more, but can be a huge time saver.

85

Multitasking is a recipe for disaster. Do **one thing at a time**. And do it well.

86

Friendly Advice

Remember the "buddy system" from summer camp? The swimming instructor would shout, "Buddies!" and you'd splash over to your buddy, join hands and raise your arms to show you were both safe. Well, grownups also need a buddy once in a while to keep them from drowning.

Every few months I get together with a group of friends. Though our ages range from 30 to 60, we're more like a pack of teenage girls as we discuss relationships, work and personal goals, all the while encouraging and validating our experiences and struggles. At the end of every visit, before we know it, hours have passed and as we say goodbye, we're already looking forward to joining hands and connecting with our buddies again.

87

Store

LIKETHINGS

together.

88

The Right Stuff

From the get-go we accumulate stuff. First comes Baby Stuff like rattles and bottles. Next, there is Childhood Stuff like Lincoln Logs, Barbie dolls and school artwork too "special" to toss. Then along comes College Stuff. Textbooks, sweatshirts and shot glasses. Those four years of further accumulation fly by faster than you can say, "Yard Sale!" and before you know it, you're schlepping that stuff home, adding it to your Younger You Stuff, and promising your parents you'll take it with you when you move out.

But adulthood is all about acquiring More Stuff (which is why you never go back for your Younger You Stuff–you don't have room) and before long Your Stuff gets entangled with your Partner's Stuff. Over the years, incrementally, if kids and pets come into the picture, Family Stuff appears.

Then one day your kids will move out (leaving Their Stuff) and that art studio you always wanted will become possible. So first you must purge the years of Collected Stuff. Eventually you pare down to just the Right Stuff–the stuff you really love–and life is great.

At least for a while.

You see, with age comes Senior Stuff and that, my friends, is a whole other story. Your art studio may need to make room for Old Age Stuff, like a walker and a stand-up chair. And it's in that stand-up chair you might spend your time looking around at Whatever Stuff is left and think, "If only I had spent more time collecting memories than stuff."

Don't let the Wrong Stuff get in the way of the Right Stuff. Get rid of it before it's too late.

89

Label all electrical charger cords, whether they're plugged in or stored in a box. That little strip of tape will save you, big time.

90

Repetition is knowledge.

(Reread this book)

From a Tiny Space to an Eviction to Coming Home

After living in that 90-square-foot apartment for awhile, I wrote an article for the New York City newspaper *Metro* about how to live comfortably in a small space. Then a reporter from the *New York Post*, having read my piece, contacted me for an article she was writing on tiny New York City apartments. The day after the *Post* piece ran, I received a Facebook message from a woman from Faircompanies.com who made videos of small homes around the world. She wanted to make a video of mine.

Kirsten arrived one humid August morning in 2010 and in less than two hours had all the footage she needed. I was in the midst of preparing for the release of my grandfather's book, *What Papa Told Me*, the cover of which happened to be on my computer screen during the shoot. After Kirsten left I didn't give the video another thought. Then, before Thanksgiving, Kirsten sent me a link to the video saying it already had 24,000 hits. I was impressed. That seemed like an awful lot.

The following April, a friend sent me a text: "Your video's on Gawker!" Then I received a call from a reporter at *The Globe and Mail* requesting an interview. Before he hung up he said, "*Globe and Mail* is the third-largest news source in the world. Your life might change after this runs."

From a YouTube video?

But of the millions of people who saw the YouTube video and the media coverage that followed, there was one person I never expected to see any of it: the apartment's landlord.

One July day I came home to find an eviction notice taped to my door. The landlord had seen the video. He knew I wasn't the woman on the lease. He wanted me out.

At the end of August, Lara, the woman I had been subletting from, and I went downtown to the New York City Housing Court. We asked the landlord's attorney if I could take over the lease. All we got was a stone-faced response: "You have to be out in a month." We didn't bring a lawyer. We thought we could talk it over. We were wrong.

When we were called up to see the judge, a clerk asked Lara, "Are you happy with this agreement?"

"No," Lara said. The clerk said we had the option to postpone the trial 30 days and negotiate for a longer stay. Lara turned to me. "Do you want to stay?"

I thought about my tiny space that had touched a nerve in millions of people around the world. "Yes," I said.

We returned to court at the end of September. While I was resigned to moving out, I was hoping for a little extra time to find a new rental. When I asked the landlord's attorney if I could at least stay through January, when rentals were more prevalent and prices lower, he said okay. Right after we signed the new agreement, the attorney cracked a smile. "I saw your video," he said. "Pretty cool."

With a deadline looming, I began running a full court press in my search for a new apartment. But the "winter thaw" that usually happened in the rental market was, for the first time in years, not happening. In fact, rents were at an all-time high, especially on the Upper West Side, where studios averaged $2,600 a month, almost four times what I was paying. And while all the studios I looked at were larger than 90 square feet, none had the charm, the sunlight or even the closet space. I wasn't yet in panic mode, but I was close.

During this time, the real estate reporter for *NY1 News* (New York City's 24-hour TV news channel) requested an interview. Since I had the studio for only another few months I figured why not? The *NY1* piece aired repeatedly over the next year. I no longer cared if the landlord saw it or not.

One day I read about a new real estate website called Streeteasy.com. I went to the site and plugged in the area I wanted to live (Upper West Side) and my price range. A half-dozen rentals popped up. I called all of them and left messages. Only one call was returned. The place was taken.

Putting aside my search, I flew down to Florida to do a few book readings with my grandfather. One day while sitting with Papa by the pool, I told him I was having a hard time finding a rental.

"Buy a place, already," Papa said, resting his hand on mine. "It's time."

When I returned to New York, I logged back on to Streeteasy.com, but this time looked up sales. When I found places in my price range, the skeptical New Yorker in me thought, "What's wrong with them?"

The first place I looked at was a one-bedroom apartment, just two blocks from my tiny studio on the same street! The location was perfect. I went to meet the realtor and arrived 10 minutes early (of course) and was greeted by a doorman (a doorman!) who told me to have a seat on a comfy leather chair in the lobby. While I waited, residents and nannies pushing strollers came and went and the doorman greeted everyone by name. It appeared to be a tight-knit community.

When the realtor arrived, the doorman whisked us

up in an old-fashioned manual-lift elevator. When I stepped out onto the seventh floor I grinned. Seven. Lucky number.

The foyer of the apartment was almost the size of the place I was vacating. A few more steps and we were inside the spacious sunny open living room/kitchen.

"All the furniture's included," the realtor said. The fact I had no furniture to speak of seemed like another good sign. At least I would have a place to sit and eat until I decided on a style.

Then I walked into the bedroom. Aside from the one deep closet and ceiling fan, there were two columns of floor-to-ceiling bookshelves bordering a large picture window with a great view and a window seat beneath. It reminded me of my childhood bedroom. *This is it*, I thought, *my new home*.

Of course when I told friends and family that I found the perfect place, everyone suggested I look at other apartments before deciding, since it was the first (and only) place I'd seen. "If only to compare," they said. So I did. I looked at larger studios with no direct sunlight and one-bedrooms with parking garages and gyms in the building. But of all the apartments, none gave me that feeling.

A few nights later I went back to that first apartment and met with the realtor. I brought a cousin in the apartment business and a family friend who owned a few properties. My cousin asked the realtor about contractors and renovations. My family friend asked about maintenance and the last time there was an increase. I asked if there was bike storage in the basement.

The next day I called my grandfather and listed the pros and cons of the apartment.

"Life is short sweetheart," said Papa, 90, a survivor of numerous near-death experiences. "Do what makes you happy."

So I put in an offer. Two months later I moved into a 490-square-foot palace. Friends joked that I wouldn't know what to do with so much space. They were half right. But what I did know was that I was determined not to fill it with stuff.

In the years since the YouTube video, I continue to receive emails from people around the world, many asking where they can find a tiny apartment like mine, as there has been an explosion in the tiny home movement. Cities from New York to San Francisco are creating small affordable spaces to fill the demand. People from coast to coast are designing and living in small homes, and many are gradually accepting the benefits of living "smaller" and are embracing the notion of having more experiences instead of more things. And while there are still plenty of folks who think I was nuts to live in such a small space, my response continues to be a simple shrug. People live in New York City for many reasons–some to follow their dreams, some for the sights, and others for the chance to become part of the energy that makes the city so exciting. We might live in our small spaces for a year, five years or forever, because our lives are more focused on enjoying life rather than on having extra square footage filled with stuff. And that, it turns out, is the grandest lesson of all.

Acknowledgments

For a relatively short book on organizing, it was a long time in the making. It changed direction a few times, and had numerous contributors who saw "organizing" along different approaches. I appreciate all those insights, because it got me to this final version. There are a few people I'd like to thank.

For starters, thank you to my Uncle Mark who not only encouraged me to move to New York City to follow my dream of becoming a writer, but also let me live with him in his small apartment (where I completely reorganized all his stuff) until I found my own footing. I can never repay you, and I will never forget what you did for me.

To Nana Banana, my paternal grandmother, thank you for instilling in me the concept that every Tupperware bottom must have a top. Your home reflected the most organized cabinets and closets in the world. I learned everything from you.

Thanks to Kirsten Dirksen from Faircompanies.com for making a wonderful YouTube video of my tiny apartment and for her large accomplishments in introducing the world to great small spaces.

To my brilliant editor and friend, Deborah Stead. Thank you for your mad skills with the red pen. I may know how to straighten up a closet, but you do the same with words.

To my father Richard Cohen, thank you for taking the time to edit and give input (more than once) and for helping me let go of words the same way I help you let go of old rusty paint cans in the garage.

To my mother Shelly Cohen, and sisters Jackie Cohen Burkey and Meredith Cohen, thank you for letting me sharpen my organizing skills on your closets. Over and over.

To my boyfriend George Casturani, thank you for your endless support, patient feedback and putting up with those never-ending comments about the loft bed.

To my blog readers, thank you for your constant supportive words, which have kept me focused on finishing this book.

And last, but certainly least, a big thanks to the landlord who evicted me from the 90-square-foot Manhattan studio apartment. If not for you, I would have never found my awesome digs. Buh-bye!

59051498R00079

Made in the USA
Charleston, SC
26 July 2016